COUNTERFEIT UNITY

A Seductive Illusion

Ralph McCall

Think Deep! Series

destinēe

THINK DEEP! SERIES

Counterfeit Unity is part of the **Think Deep! Series**, created for those who want more than surface answers.

Each book in the series explores the big questions about culture, identity, and faith—designed for a digital generation immersed in an endless array of perspectives and ever-shifting narratives.

To develop true and just discernment.

COPYRIGHT

Counterfeit Unity: A Seductive Illusion
By Ralph McCall

© Copyright 2025 by Ralph McCall

All rights reserved. No part of this publication may be reproduced, distributed, or transmitted in any form or by any means, including photocopying, recording, or other electronic or mechanical methods, without the prior written permission of the publisher, except in the case of brief quotations embodied in critical reviews and certain other noncommercial uses permitted by copyright law.

Scripture quotations are from the ESV® Bible (The Holy Bible, English Standard Version®), copyright © 2001 by Crossway Bibles, a publishing ministry of Good News Publishers. Used by permission. All rights reserved.

Published by Destinee Media, www.destineemedia.com
Written by Ralph McCall
ISBN: 978-1-938367-93-9

CONTENTS

THINK DEEP! SERIES iii
Copyright iv
Contents v
Introduction: Why Unity Feels Good but is fragile 1
Part I: The Foundation Is Cracked 4
Chapter 1: The Paradox of Unity 5
Chapter 2: When Feelings Pretend to Be God 10
Chapter 3: The Illusion of "All Is One" 15
Chapter 4: What Is Truth, Really? 20
Chapter 5: The Cult of Unity 24
Chapter 6: When Unity Kills Discernment 28
Chapter 7: The Idol of Inclusion 33
Part II: The Way Back to Real Unity 38
Chapter 8: Testing the Spirits (Even the Trendy Ones) 39
Chapter 9: When Spirituality Poses as Truth 44
Chapter 10: Real Unity in Christ 49
Chapter 11: Love That Doesn't Lie 54
Chapter 12: What Do We Unify On? 62
Epilogue: What We've Seen—and What Comes Next 67
Annotated Bibliography 71
For Further Reading 74

INTRODUCTION: WHY UNITY FEELS GOOD BUT IS FRAGILE

A pervasive idea has crept into our culture—it's flawed — and it's probably already in your group chat. It presents itself under the label of **"unity"**.

This book is here to unmask it, and help you escape it.

You've probably felt it.

That awkward silence in a group chat when someone dares to bring up faith or morality. That pressure in a classroom or workplace to nod along, even when you disagree. That moment in church when the sermon sounds more like a motivational talk than a message from God. You know that moment. You just finished typing a sincere, thoughtful opinion on a moral issue, hit 'send,' and immediately regretted it.

It's the same message everywhere: ***"Don't divide. Don't offend. Just love and accept everyone."***

It sounds beautiful. It feels safe. It promises peace, and even better, social approval.

But here's the problem: it doesn't last.

- Friendships fracture the moment someone speaks an unpopular truth.
- Churches drift when "unity" becomes more important than holiness.
- Your own faith feels shaky when you're told to keep convictions private.

You're left wondering: *Why does unity feel so fragile? Why does "love" often mean silence? Why does peace collapse the moment truth shows up?*

This book is about those questions.

Because what you're experiencing isn't random—it's the result of a worldview shaping our culture, our churches, and even our own hearts. A worldview that whispers: *"All is One. Truth is personal. Conviction is dangerous. Inclusion is everything."*

This is the result of a worldview we'll call **Therapeutic Cohesion**. It's when the group decides that feeling comfy and affirmed is the main goal, so we all have to dodge the tough, messy truths. It basically trades **real unity** for **zero drama**.

It promises belonging. But it delivers confusion. It looks like love. But it leaves you empty. It feels like peace. But it's counterfeit.

Why This Book Matters for You

If you've ever:

- Felt pressured to stay silent so you wouldn't be labeled "divisive."
- Wondered why "truth" sounds harsh but "affirmation" gets applause.
- Longed for real community but found shallow belonging.

Then this book is for you.

You don't need another pep talk about being nice. You need clarity. You need courage. You need to know what real unity is—and what it isn't.

What You'll Discover

In these pages, we'll unmask the counterfeits:

- Unity built on vibes instead of truth.
- Love redefined as affirmation.
- Inclusion that opens the door to deception.
- Spirituality that feels powerful but denies Christ.

And we'll rediscover the real thing:

- Unity anchored in truth.
- Love that doesn't lie.
- Inclusion that transforms, not just affirms.
- A foundation strong enough to hold your faith when culture shifts again.

You'll find out why Counterfeit Unity is a seductive illusion.

The Invitation

This isn't just a cultural critique. It's a roadmap back to reality. Back to clarity. Back to Christ.

Because the world doesn't need more shallow belonging. It needs the kind of unity Jesus prayed for—the kind that costs something, but lasts forever.

So here's the question: Will you settle for counterfeit unity that feels good but fades? Or will you step into the costly clarity of Christ, where truth and love finally meet?

Let's find out.

PART I: THE FOUNDATION IS CRACKED

How Postmodern Oneness Became a False Gospel

CHAPTER 1: THE PARADOX OF UNITY

When Everyone's "Truth" Cancels Out Everyone Else's

Unity is one of the most celebrated words of our time. It's painted on protest signs, hash-tagged on social media, and preached from pulpits. Politicians invoke it, influencers market it, and churches sing about it. The word itself feels safe, warm, and unthreatening. Who could be against unity?

But beneath the glow of the word lies a paradox. The more our culture talks about unity, the less united we actually are. The louder the calls for harmony, the more fragile our relationships become. The more we insist on "inclusion," the more suspicious we grow of anyone who dares to disagree.

This paradox is not accidental. It is the fruit of a deep shift in how Western culture thinks about truth, meaning, and belonging. To understand why unity has become so fragile, we need to trace the ideas that have shaped the air we breathe.

The Suspicion of Truth

For centuries, Western thought assumed that truth was something objective—something "out there" that could be discovered, debated, and shared. But in the last hundred years, that assumption has been dismantled.

The philosopher Friedrich Nietzsche declared that "God is dead," not as a celebration of atheism, but as a recognition that Western culture no longer believed in a transcendent source of truth. If there is no God, then truth is not revealed—it is constructed.

This suspicion of truth deepened in the twentieth century with **Postmodernism**. Postmodern thinkers argued that truth is not universal but personal. Instead of asking, *"What is true for everyone?"* the question became, *"What's true for me?"*

Then came **Deconstructionism**, which claimed that truth itself is a tool of power. Words don't reveal reality, they manipulate it. Every sermon, every law, every tradition is just a mask for control.

The result is a culture where everyone has "their truth," but no one is allowed to claim *the* truth. And if truth divides, then truth must be silenced.

The New Unity Creed

Into this vacuum stepped a new creed, one that feels noble and compassionate:

"Love and accept everyone."

It's the motto of our age. It appears on Instagram posts, in classroom discussions, and even in church slogans. It sounds like the perfect solution to division. If truth is too divisive, then unity must be built on acceptance.

But this creed comes with a hidden cost. If unity means unconditional acceptance, then discernment disappears. To question someone's belief is to disrupt the harmony. To draw boundaries is to offend. To speak truth is to divide.

Unity becomes less about what is real and more about what feels safe. It's not built on conviction but on silence. It's not forged through truth but through avoidance and suppression. And it not only happens in the general culture, but also in churches that sing about belonging while quietly pressuring members never to raise hard questions.

This is why our culture can chant "unity" while splintering into tribes. Look around. Polarization is the reality rather than universal unity. The All is One mantra can't hold. It's why people can post about love while canceling those who disagree. What looks like unity is often just conformity.

Schaeffer's Two Beginnings

Here's where philosopher/theologian Francis Schaeffer helps us. He argued that every worldview begins with one of two starting points. And whichever beginning you choose determines how you answer life's biggest questions.

1. **An Impersonal Beginning**
    - The universe began with blind forces, random energy, or indifferent matter.
    - There is no Designer, no intention, no moral direction.
    - You are just atoms with Wi-Fi.
    - In this framework:
        - **Meaning** is an illusion.
        - **Identity** is fluid, because nothing defines you beyond your feelings.
        - **Love** is just a chemical impulse, not an ultimate reality.
        - **Unity** is social convenience—staying together as long as it feels good, as long as we don't self-destruct.

2. **A Personal Beginning**
    - The universe began with a Creator—intelligent, moral, relational.
    - You were made on purpose, by Someone who knows you.
    - In this framework:
        - **Meaning** is real, because it flows from design.
        - **Identity** is secure, because it's rooted in something greater than yourself.

- **Love** is ultimate, because it comes from a personal source.
- **Unity** is possible, because it's grounded in truth, not just feelings.

The "All is One" worldview tries to live in the first story (impersonal beginnings) while borrowing the benefits of the second (personal meaning). It wants love, justice, and unity—but without a personal God to ground them. That's why it collapses. It's a house without a foundation.

The Seductive Illusion

This counterfeit unity is fragile because it cannot survive disagreement. It thrives only as long as no one asks hard questions. It looks strong in moments of shared emotion—at a rally, in a group chat, during a worship song—but it collapses the moment truth enters the room.

Philosopher Alasdair MacIntyre observed that modern culture has "lost our comprehension, both theoretical and practical, of morality." Without a shared foundation of truth, unity becomes impossible. All that's left is a seductive illusion, held together by vibes and slogans.

And yet, people cling to it. Why? Because the alternative—living with the emptiness of an impersonal beginning—is unbearable. We cannot live without meaning, belonging, and love. So we settle for a counterfeit version, one that feels real in the moment but fades as soon as the music stops or the conversation gets uncomfortable.

Where This Leads

This is the paradox of unity in our time: the more we chase it apart from truth, the less we actually find it. The more we silence disagreement in the name of peace, the more fragile our peace is.

But counterfeit unity doesn't just shape how we think. It shapes how we live. It drives us to seek belonging in festivals, in group chats, in curated online communities, and even in worship services where emotion becomes the substitute for truth.

That's where we must go next. Because counterfeit unity cannot survive on ideas alone. It needs something more—something to give it the appearance of meaning. And in our culture, that "something" is almost always emotion.

If Chapter 1 exposes the paradox of counterfeit unity and its philosophical roots, Chapter 2 will show how it survives. We'll see why counterfeit unity leans so heavily on emotional highs—whether in concerts, group chats, or even church worship—and why this dependence reveals its emptiness.

CHAPTER 2: WHEN FEELINGS PRETEND TO BE GOD

Why Counterfeit Unity Needs Emotional Highs to Survive

The festival ends. The group chat goes silent. The unity fades. But the hunger for belonging doesn't.

We can't live in the emptiness that "everyone has their truth" leaves behind. It's too thin, too fragile, too hollow. So we reach for something more—something that feels transcendent.

For some, it's the next concert, the next protest, the next viral trend. For others, it's the next worship set, the next conference, the next moment when the lights dim and the music swells. In both cases, the logic is the same: if truth is too divisive, then feelings must be the voice of God.

This is how counterfeit unity survives. It cannot stand on reason or truth, so it props itself up with emotion.

The Festival Effect

At a music festival, thousands of strangers sway to the same beat. For a moment, it feels like everyone is one. The lights, the rhythm, the crowd—it's intoxicating. You feel connected to people you've never met, as if you're part of something bigger.

But the next morning, the feeling fades. The crowd disperses. The unity is gone. What seemed like transcendence was just adrenaline and ambience.

That's how counterfeit unity works. It thrives on shared vibes, not shared truth. It feels powerful, but it collapses as soon as the music stops.

The Group Chat Illusion

The same pattern shows up in smaller spaces. In your group chat, everyone's laughing at the same memes, sharing playlists, hyping each other up. It feels like you're all on the same wavelength—until someone brings up politics, faith, or morality. Suddenly, the vibe shifts. Someone goes silent. Someone leaves.

Counterfeit unity survives only as long as no one asks hard questions. It's peace by avoidance. It's harmony by silence.

The Worship Service Mirage

And here's where it gets uncomfortable. The same counterfeit pattern can show up in church.

When the lights dim, the music swells, and the crowd lifts their hands, it can feel like God is speaking. But sometimes, what we're experiencing isn't His voice—it's the atmosphere.

When emotion becomes the foundation, worship risks turning into **emotional gnosticism**—the belief that spiritual highs equal divine truth. In this system, the goal isn't to know God through His Word, but to feel Him through the music. And there must always be a new higher-high.

It looks like unity. Everyone's singing the same song. Everyone's moved to tears. But if the foundation is mostly emotion, then the unity is counterfeit. It's not the Spirit leading—it's the vibe.

Why We Do This

No one can live consistently with emptiness. If truth is silenced, if convictions are privatized, if meaning is dismantled, then something has to fill the void. And in our culture, that "something" is almost always emotion.

We borrow transcendence from the atmosphere. We smuggle in meaning through goosebumps. We pretend that the euphoria of a crowd or the tears in a worship set are proof of reality. It's a survival strategy. Without truth, we lean on feelings. Without foundations, we lean on vibes.

So, let's dig deeper into why this happens. We didn't arrive here by accident. Postmodernism told us there is no absolute truth—only personal perspectives. Deconstructionism went further, insisting that words themselves are slippery, masks for power rather than carriers of meaning. Put those together, and what's left? At best, I can cling to "my truth," but it floats without anchor. It isn't *the* truth, built on a foundation that can actually hold. And when truth is dismantled, all I have left to lean on is experience—whatever feels real in the moment.

The Psychology of Counterfeit Unity

Why does this work so well? Because emotions are powerful. They bypass the intellect and go straight to the heart. They create a sense of immediacy, of authenticity.

- **Emotions feel real.** When you're moved to tears, it feels like truth.
- **Emotions feel unifying.** When everyone in the room is crying, it feels like you're all one.
- **Emotions feel safe.** They don't demand definitions, boundaries, or confrontation.

But here's the catch: emotions are real, but they're not always reliable. They can point to truth, but they can also be manipulated.

They can confirm reality, but they can also create illusions.

That's why counterfeit unity leans so heavily on them. Because if you can't build on truth, you have to build on something. And feelings are the easiest substitute.

The Cost of Emotional Unity

But here's the danger: when feelings pretend to be God, discernment disappears.

- Harmful ideas slip in because they "feel right."
- False teachers gain influence because they "sound inspiring."
- Churches drift because they confuse atmosphere with anointing.

Counterfeit unity can't survive without emotional highs. But emotional highs can't sustain a soul.

Borrowed Meaning

The "All is One" worldview is unlivable. Left alone, it collapses into despair. To avoid that despair, we prop it up with feelings—festivals, events, group chats, worship vibes. But that's not real unity. It's borrowed meaning. It's a counterfeit voice of God.

The question is not whether emotion is bad. It's whether emotion is enough. And if unity is built only on what we feel, then it will collapse the moment those feelings fade.

A Generation at Risk

Gen-Z and Millennials are especially vulnerable here. Raised in a world of curated experiences, algorithm-driven feeds, and therapeutic language, they've been taught to trust feelings above all else.

- If it resonates, it must be true.
- If it feels safe, it must be good.
- If it feels unifying, it must be right.

But this is a dangerous equation. Because what resonates isn't always true. What feels safe isn't always good. And what feels unifying isn't always right.

This leads to the problem of trust and suspicion – our emotions and feelings might be deceiving us. So, self-deception is at the heart of the issue. Lots of people never consider that they might be deceived by themselves, leading to a suspicion, not just of others, but of oneself,

Without discernment, a generation raised on sensations will mistake counterfeit unity for the real thing.

Counterfeit unity thrives on emotion, but emotion alone cannot explain why it fails so quickly. To understand the deeper problem, we need to look at the worldview beneath it—the philosophy that whispers through our culture: *"All is One."*

That's where we turn next.

CHAPTER 3: THE ILLUSION OF "ALL IS ONE"

Why the Dream of Getting Along Breaks Down Without Truth

Unity feels right. It feels like the answer to everything that's broken.

We hear it everywhere:

- "We're all one."
- "Let's stop judging and just love."
- "Everyone belongs, no matter what they believe."

For many in Gen-Z and Millennial circles, this isn't just social etiquette—it's a moral absolute. It feels like the antidote to division, injustice, and loneliness. If we could just agree to be kind, maybe the world would stop tearing itself apart. Maybe relationships wouldn't keep collapsing. Maybe the church wouldn't keep dividing. Maybe your own life would feel more settled.

Unity feels like the cure. But if it's really that powerful, why does everything still feel so fractured? Why do movements built on togetherness keep breaking apart? Why do friendships collapse after a disagreement on politics or theology? Why does "just love people" turn into "just cancel them" the moment someone offends?

The answer is simple but sobering: **unity without truth doesn't hold.** It breaks under pressure. And the deeper reason for this fracture is philosophical. It's not just that we disagree—it's that we've been trained to see reality through a lens that makes disagreement intolerable and truth negotiable.

The Philosophy Beneath the Slogans

What most people call "unity" today isn't just a social idea. It's spiritual. It's metaphysical. It's the belief that at the deepest level of reality, there are no real distinctions. Everything is divine. Everything is energy. Everything is one.

This is the core of the **Oneness worldview**—a modern remix of ancient ideas drawn from Hinduism, Buddhism, Gnostic mysticism, and New Age thought. But now, it's gone viral.

You've probably heard it in phrases like:

- "The universe has your back."
- "God is in everything."
- "Raise your vibration."
- "You just need to align with your higher self."

At first glance, this doesn't sound toxic. It sounds peaceful. It promises harmony without conflict, spirituality without dogma, belonging without boundaries.

But this worldview doesn't just change how we relate to each other—it redefines reality itself.

If "all is one," then:

- **Truth** is not objective—it's just your perspective.
- **Identity** is not rooted—it's whatever you feel today.
- **God** is not a person to know—but a presence to feel.
- **Salvation** is not rescue—but awakening to what's already within you.

It sounds unifying. But it slowly erases the lines that make love meaningful, truth possible, and justice real.

As theologian Albert Mohler warns: *"Pantheism dissolves the distinctions that make moral knowledge and redemption possible. When God is everything, God is nothing in particular."*

Why "Oneness" Feels Good

Let's be real—Oneness doesn't sound threatening. It sounds like healing. It promises:

- An end to religious conflict.
- A break from judgmental people.
- A spirituality that's flexible, soothing, and non-demanding.
- No more divisions. No more dogma. Just ambience.

And for a generation burned by hypocrisy, scandals, and endless arguments, that's appealing. Who wouldn't want a spirituality that feels safe, inclusive, and affirming?

But here's the catch: **when you remove truth, you remove boundaries.** And when you remove boundaries, the lines don't just shift—they vanish. "Love" means avoiding offense. "Peace" means staying silent. "Unity" means agreeing never to disagree.

The Collapse of Distinctions

The Oneness worldview collapses because it erases the very distinctions that make unity meaningful.

- If everything is one, then good and evil are illusions.
- If everything is one, then justice and injustice are indistinguishable.
- If everything is one, then love is just self-affirmation.

Think about it: if there's no difference between light and darkness, then light loses its meaning. If there's no difference between truth and lies, then truth becomes irrelevant. If there's no difference between God and creation, then God becomes unnecessary.

The result is not harmony—it's confusion. Not peace, but silence. Not unity, but conformity.

From Oneness to Counterfeit Unity

Here's how the logic of Oneness becomes the gospel of Counterfeit Unity:

1. If all is one, then there are no ultimate distinctions.
2. If there are no ultimate distinctions, then no belief can be considered invalid.
3. If no belief can be considered invalid, then unity is defined as affirming all beliefs.
4. If unity is defined as affirming all beliefs, then rejecting or critiquing a belief is considered offensive.
5. If truth claims are considered offensive, then truth must be silenced to preserve unity.

Conclusion: If all is one, truth must be silenced.

It's a slow slide—from open-mindedness to enforced silence. And once we reach the bottom, we're not united—we're just muted.

The Hidden Cost

The "All is One" philosophy promises unity, but it delivers counterfeit harmony. It offers belonging, but only if you never challenge the group. It offers peace, but only if you silence your convictions. It offers love, but only if you redefine love as unconditional affirmation.

It's unity without truth. And unity without truth isn't unity at all—it's control.

The Oneness worldview sounds compassionate, but it cannot sustain real unity. It collapses because it begins with the wrong foundation—an impersonal beginning that cannot account for meaning, identity, love, or justice.

To see why, we need to go deeper. We need to ask the most basic question of all: *What if there is truth outside yourself?* Because how you answer that question determines everything else.

That's where we turn next.

CHAPTER 4: WHAT IS TRUTH, REALLY?

Why Real Unity Requires Something More Than Just "Your Truth"

Truth. It's a word we throw around constantly, but rarely stop to define.

Scroll through your feed and you'll see it everywhere:

- "Speak your truth."
- "Live your truth."
- "Find your truth."

It sounds empowering. It sounds authentic. But it also raises a question: if everyone has their own truth, does truth even exist anymore?

This is not just a word game. Your definition of truth shapes your entire life. It determines how you see yourself, how you treat others, and what kind of unity you think is possible. And right now, our culture is deeply confused about it.

Two Definitions. Two Destinies.

There are really only two competing definitions of truth in play today. And they flow directly from the two worldviews we explored in a previous chapter: the **impersonal beginning** and the **personal beginning**.

1. **Truth in the Cult of Unity: "There is no truth—only perspective."** This is the Postmodern definition, born from the Oneness worldview. If everything is one, if distinctions are illusions, then truth can't be absolute. It's just personal. It's just preference.

In this view:

- Truth is relative.
- Reality is subjective.
- "You do you" becomes sacred wisdom.
- "What's true for you is true for you, and what's true for me is true for me."

It sounds freeing. No hard boundaries. No absolutes. No conflict.

But here's the problem: when everything is true… nothing really is.

You can't live this out consistently.

- **Medicine:** "I don't need surgery. I'm manifesting my healing." But belief doesn't stop a tumor from growing.
- **Justice:** "In my truth, I didn't steal anything—even if the security footage says otherwise." Try that in court.
- **Engineering:** "My truth says this bridge is safe, even though the supports are cracked." Belief doesn't make it structurally sound.
- **Morality:** "In my truth, this isn't wrong—it's just misunderstood." When morality becomes relative, anything can be justified. Abuse becomes "freedom." Corruption becomes "strategy." Evil hides behind "my truth." It's okay to take the life of someone who disagrees with me.

If right and wrong are just a matter of perspective, then who decides what justice is? If everyone gets to invent their own compass, then no one has the authority to say murder is wrong, racism is evil, or exploitation is unjust.

As Ravi Zacharias once pointed out: *"When you say there is no such thing as truth, you're asking me to believe you—while denying that truth exists."*

That's the contradiction at the heart of counterfeit unity. It silences truth in the name of peace, but in doing so, it destroys the very foundation of peace.

2. **Truth in the Biblical Worldview: "Truth is what aligns with God's reality."** If the universe begins not with impersonal energy, but with a personal God, then truth is not just possible—it's knowable.

In this view:

- Truth is absolute—not flexible.
- Truth is discovered—not invented.
- Truth is loving—even when it confronts.

Truth doesn't float in space—it flows from the character of God. Truth is outside yourself.

Jesus said: *"I am the way, the truth, and the life. No one comes to the Father except through me."* (John 14:6)

That means truth is not just a concept—it's a Person. It's relational. It's embodied.

And the result? *"You shall know the truth, and the truth shall make you free."* (John 8:32)

This is truth that doesn't shift with your mood. It doesn't silence hard questions—it answers them with clarity. It doesn't just affirm—it transforms.

As Kevin DeYoung puts it: *"You can have truth without unity (and that's a problem), but you can't have unity without truth—not real unity."*

Carl Trueman is even more blunt: *"The modern quest for community apart from truth is doomed to either tyranny or chaos."*

Translation: if your unity can't survive one person

disagreeing with the group chat, it's not unity—it's peer pressure in skinny jeans.

Why This Matters

Truth isn't the enemy of unity. It's the foundation of it.

Without truth, love has no backbone. Justice has no anchor. Unity has no foundation.

Our culture claims there's no such thing as absolute truth. But ironically, "unity" has become the new absolute—the one belief no one is allowed to challenge.

So the real question is this: **What kind of unity are you chasing? And what is it built on?**

Counterfeit unity doesn't unite you to truth—it disconnects you from reality. Real unity requires something more. It requires truth that is bigger than you, outside of you, and strong enough to hold you together when everything else falls apart.

We've seen how counterfeit unity silences truth, and how real unity requires it. But our culture doesn't just misunderstand truth—it worships unity itself. Unity has become a god, demanding sacrifice. And that's where we turn next.

CHAPTER 5: THE CULT OF UNITY

When Belonging Becomes Bondage

Unity is no longer just a value in our culture—it has become a religion.

It has its own creed: *"Love and accept everyone."* It has its own rituals: hashtags, slogans, curated aesthetics. It has its own high priests: influencers, activists, even pastors who preach belonging without boundaries. And like every religion, it has its own god.

That god is **Unity itself**. And like every false god, it demands sacrifice.

The God of Belonging

Let's be honest: everyone wants to belong. We crave connection. We fear isolation. We long for community. That longing is good—it's part of how we were created. But when belonging becomes the highest good, it turns into bondage.

In today's culture, unity is treated as sacred. The worst sin is not lying, cheating, or even harming others. The worst sin is *dividing*. To disagree is to disrupt. To draw boundaries is to betray. To speak truth is to wound the god of unity. So we learn the rules:

- You can believe whatever you want—just don't say it's true for everyone.
- You can speak your mind—just don't challenge the group.
- You can follow Jesus—just don't claim He's the only way.

This isn't unity. It's compliance. It's not love. It's fear dressed up as compassion.

Culture as Discipleship

Here's the thing about culture: it doesn't just entertain you. It disciples you.

Culture tells you what's normal, what's offensive, what's safe, and what's sacred. And it does it so subtly you don't even notice. You scroll, you laugh, you nod along—and slowly, you're being formed.

As anthropologist Clifford Geertz once said, culture is like a web of meaning we spin around ourselves until we forget we're caught in it.

That's why counterfeit unity feels so natural. It doesn't feel like pressure. It feels like truth. It feels like kindness. It feels like love. But it's not. It's formation without foundation.

The Demands of the Cult

Every false god demands sacrifice. The Cult of Unity is no different.

- **Sacrifice your convictions.** Don't say what you believe if it might offend.
- **Sacrifice your clarity.** Keep your words vague so no one feels excluded.
- **Sacrifice your courage.** Stay silent when you should speak.
- **Sacrifice your faith.** Privatize it. Keep it personal. Don't bring it into the public square.

The Cult of Unity whispers: *"If you want to belong, you must bow."*

And many do. They trade conviction for consensus, truth for tolerance, and courage for comfort.

The Trap of Inclusion Without Discernment

In this cult, inclusion is sacred. But it's not real inclusion. It's not "come as you are and be transformed." It's "come as you are and stay as you are."

That sounds compassionate, but it's actually cruel. Because if nothing ever changes, then nothing ever heals. If no one ever confronts, then no one ever grows.

This is why counterfeit unity is so dangerous in the church. When inclusion is elevated above discernment, false teaching slips in unnoticed. Harmful ideas are tolerated in the name of love. Leaders are celebrated for charisma instead of character. And slowly, the church loses its immune system.

As Carl Trueman warns: *"A culture that elevates consensus over conviction will always crucify the truth-teller."*

The Illusion of Peace

The Cult of Unity promises peace. But it's a fragile peace—the kind that only lasts as long as no one asks hard questions.

It's the peace of the group chat where no one mentions politics. It's the peace of the church where no one preaches repentance. It's the peace of the family dinner where no one talks about faith.

It feels safe. But it's hollow. Because peace without truth isn't peace—it's denial.

Jesus Himself said: *"Do not think that I have come to bring peace to the earth. I have not come to bring peace, but a sword."* (Matthew 10:34)

That doesn't mean He came to divide for the sake of division. It means He came to bring truth. And truth always divides before it unites. It cuts through lies, exposes sin, and calls people to repentance. Only then can real peace be built.

Think About This

- Have you ever stayed silent to keep the peace, even when you knew you should speak?
- Have you confused kindness with compliance?
- Have you traded conviction for consensus?

If so, you've felt the pull of the Cult of Unity.

Conclusion: Breaking Free

The Cult of Unity is powerful because it taps into a real longing—the longing to belong. But it twists that longing into bondage. It demands silence, compliance, and compromise.

Real unity doesn't demand your silence. It doesn't erase your convictions. It doesn't crucify truth-tellers. Real unity is built on truth, sustained by grace, and anchored in Christ.

The Cult of Unity says: *"Bow to belong."* Jesus says: *"You shall know the truth, and the truth shall set you free."*

If unity itself has become a god, then it's no surprise that discernment is treated as a threat. In the next chapter, we'll see how counterfeit unity doesn't just silence truth—it kills the very ability to think critically.

CHAPTER 6: WHEN UNITY KILLS DISCERNMENT

How Counterfeit Unity Robs You of Critical Thinking

Unity is supposed to be a strength. But when unity is built on silence instead of truth, it becomes a trap. And one of the first casualties is **discernment**.

Discernment is the ability to tell the difference between what is true and what only looks true. It's the spiritual immune system of the church and the individual believer. Without it, you can't tell the difference between medicine and poison, between a shepherd and a wolf, between the Spirit of God and the spirit of the age.

But counterfeit unity doesn't want you to discern. It wants you to stop asking questions, stop testing ideas, stop thinking critically. Because the moment you do, the illusion of peace begins to crack.

When Thinking Becomes a Threat

Have you ever noticed how quickly a room can go cold when someone asks a hard question? Maybe you quoted Scripture in a small group and suddenly the conversation got awkward. Maybe you raised a concern about a popular teaching and were told you were being "divisive."

It's subtle, but it's everywhere. We're being trained to believe that thinking deeply is dangerous, that discernment is just judgment in disguise, that theology is a barrier to community instead of its foundation.

This is what counterfeit unity does to your mind. It doesn't just reshape your beliefs—it deactivates the part of you that's meant to wrestle, test, and anchor your faith in truth.

Nancy Pearcey once wrote: *"The most dangerous ideas in a society are not the ones being argued, but the ones that are assumed."*

Counterfeit unity thrives on assumptions. It doesn't need to shout you down. It just needs you to stop thinking.

The Slow Death of Discernment

The Bible never tells us to check our brains at the door for the sake of peace. In fact, it commands the opposite:

- *"Do not be conformed to this world, but be transformed by the renewal of your mind."* (Romans 12:2)
- *"Test everything; hold fast what is good."* (1 Thessalonians 5:21)
- *"Take every thought captive to obey Christ."* (2 Corinthians 10:5)

Discernment is not optional—it's obedience.

But counterfeit unity whispers a different creed:

- Don't test—just trust.
- Don't think—just feel.
- Don't question—just agree.

Over time, this doesn't just dull your mind. It destabilizes your soul. Because when truth becomes taboo, lies become sacred.

How We Got Numb

Let's be honest: most of us were raised to believe that hurting someone's feelings is worse than being wrong. We've been trained—through influencers, TED Talks, social justice slogans, and even church culture—that kindness means avoiding discomfort.

And so, we adapted.

- We stopped asking deep questions so we wouldn't be labeled "divisive."
- We avoided talking about sin because it felt "negative."
- We backed off from spiritual conversations unless they were cozy and universal.

Slowly, we began to equate silence with compassion.

But silence isn't always love. Sometimes it's fear.

C.S. Lewis once said: *"God is no fonder of intellectual slackers than of any other slackers."*

You were never meant to check your brain at the church door—or at the feet of culture.

The Lie: "If You Think Too Much, You'll Divide Us"

Here's how this mindset sneaks in:

- Thinking deeply is seen as being "too intense."
- Conviction is mistaken for arrogance.
- Theological clarity is brushed off as "just your take."
- Discernment is framed as dangerous or even as "religious trauma."

But disagreement isn't trauma. It's part of discipleship.

Truth isn't unkind. It's what sets you free.

If your community can't handle being lovingly challenged, that's not unity—it's groupthink. And if you're afraid to speak truth because it might upset the balance, that's not peace—it's fear in a spiritual costume.

How It Affects You

When you let counterfeit unity dictate the boundaries of your mind, here's what happens—quietly, slowly, but inevitably:

- You avoid Scripture unless it "feels relevant" or inspirational.
- You rely on emotions to decide if something is true.
- You quote Christian influencers more than you quote the Bible.
- You interpret "peace" as agreement, not as confidence in God's truth.

The end result? You may feel connected, but you'll be confused. You'll go with the crowd, but not with Christ. You'll protect unity—and lose your clarity.

Real Unity Doesn't Fear Truth

Here's what the early church knew—and what we need to reclaim:

- Loving someone means correcting them (Galatians 6:1).
- Faith involves both heart and mind (Matthew 22:37).
- Spiritual maturity requires testing, not just trusting your gut (Hebrews 5:14).

Jesus never called us to drift with the culture. He called us to renew our minds, to love Him with all our heart, soul, and intellect.

And you don't need a seminary degree to think critically. You just need to stop outsourcing your convictions to culture—or to comfort.

Think About This

- Have you ever stayed silent just to avoid sounding "too religious"?
- Have you confused kindness with never disagreeing?
- Do you actually know what you believe—or just what your friends believe?

Discernment isn't arrogance. It's obedience.

Conclusion: The Courage to Test

Counterfeit unity kills discernment because it knows discernment is dangerous to its survival. The moment you start testing, the illusion cracks. The moment you start thinking, the silence breaks.

Real unity doesn't fear truth. It welcomes it. It tests everything, holds fast to what is good, and throws out what is false.

Because unity without discernment isn't unity at all—it's surrender.

If counterfeit unity kills discernment, then it's no surprise that inclusion becomes the new idol. In the next chapter, we'll see how "welcoming everyone" without boundaries isn't the gospel—it's another mask for counterfeit unity.

CHAPTER 7: THE IDOL OF INCLUSION

When "Welcoming Everyone" Without Discernment Isn't the Gospel

---

The Kind of Love That Doesn't Heal

You've heard the lines. Maybe you've even said them.

"Everyone is welcome here."

"This is a safe space—no judgment."

They sound Christlike. Compassionate. Irresistibly comforting.

But here's the question almost no one asks: **Is it still the Gospel if it never calls anyone to change?**

Today's culture has turned "love" into a soft glow that affirms everything and confronts nothing. In this vision of inclusion, boundaries feel offensive, and truth feels like hate speech. We're told that saying "this is wrong" is worse than the thing itself.

But that's not what love does.

Love that only affirms is like a doctor who hugs you and refuses to tell you you're dying. It may feel safe in the moment—but it can't save you.

As D.A. Carson reminds us: *"People do not drift toward holiness... We drift toward compromise."*

How Inclusion Became the New Gospel

For Gen-Z and Millennials, inclusion isn't just a virtue—it's the litmus test of morality. If you aren't inclusive, you must be oppressive. If you say someone's lifestyle needs transformation, you're a bigot. The highest good today isn't holiness—it's affirmation.

This version of Christianity doesn't say, "Come to Jesus and be changed." It says, "Come as you are—and stay as you are."

Why does it feel so right? Because it's reacting to real wounds:

- Churches that preached legalism but showed no grace.
- Leaders who used doctrine as a hammer, not a guide.
- Christians who confused holiness with hostility.

In reaction to these errors, we built an idol: the **God of Nice.** He never offends. Never confronts. Never contradicts.

And slowly, a therapeutic gospel took the place of the biblical one.

Carl Trueman observes: *"In our culture, the notion of morality has been replaced by a sense of psychological well-being."*

When the Cult of Unity Disarms Your Discernment

Here's where things get dangerous. The Cult of Unity tells you to silence conviction for the sake of emotional peace. But when that happens—when critical thinking is shut down and all inclusion is sacred—you become vulnerable to deception.

Without discernment:

- You start inviting destructive worldviews into your soul—because they sound spiritual.

- You start tolerating distorted gospels in your church—because they seem welcoming.
- You lose the ability to say "this is not from God."

If every belief is welcome, eventually so is every false teacher. And if there's no line to draw—where does it stop?

Paul warned the Galatians with razor-sharp clarity: *"If anyone is preaching to you a gospel contrary to the one you received, let him be accursed."* (Galatians 1:9)

Today's inclusive gospel wouldn't dare say that. It doesn't curse false gospels—it compliments them. It doesn't name deception—it normalizes it.

When inclusion becomes your idol, you stop guarding your soul.

The Real Jesus Welcomed Sinners—but Confronted Sin

Let's be clear: Jesus was radically inclusive. He touched lepers. He dined with tax collectors. He broke social rules to meet people where they were. But He never left them there.

- To the woman caught in adultery: *"Go, and sin no more."*
- To Zacchaeus: *"Salvation has come"*— after radical repentance.
- To the rich young ruler: *"Sell everything and follow me"*— turn away from materialism to the true God.

Inclusion was the door. Repentance was the path. Transformation was the destination.

Jesus never used grace to dodge truth. He used truth to bring grace to life.

As Rosaria Butterfield puts it: *"Love that goes silent in the face of sin is not love. It is cowardice."*

The Lie: "To Love Me, You Must Agree With Me"

This is the beating heart of the Cult of Unity. If you don't affirm me, you disrespect me. If you challenge me, you reject me. If you name sin, you're dangerous.

But Scripture says the opposite:

- *"Faithful are the wounds of a friend."* (Proverbs 27:6)
- *"Speak the truth in love."* (Ephesians 4:15)
- *"Correct with gentleness."* (2 Timothy 2:25)

In a world where affirmation has replaced love, correction feels like violence. But that's what makes real love so rare—and so needed. It tells the truth, even when it costs you everything.

Think About This

- Have you started avoiding hard truths because you fear being labeled "unloving"?
- Have you assumed that kindness = silence?
- Has your church traded the cross for a couch?

Let's say it plainly: **A gospel that doesn't call for repentance isn't the Gospel.**

It's a motivational speech with a halo filter.

The Gospel welcomes sinners. But it never leaves them in their sin.

Conclusion: Inclusion Without Transformation Is Counterfeit

The idol of inclusion promises safety, but it delivers stagnation. It offers belonging, but without boundaries. It offers love, but without truth.

Real inclusion is not the absence of confrontation—it's the presence of transformation. Jesus welcomes you as you are, but He loves you too much to leave you there.

Counterfeit unity says: *"Stay comfortable."* The Gospel says: *"Be changed."*

If inclusion without discernment is an idol, then the next step is clear: we must recover the ability to test what is spiritual. Because not everything that feels spiritual is from God. That's where we turn next.

PART II: THE WAY BACK TO REAL UNITY

Recovering the Only Foundation Strong Enough to Unite Us

CHAPTER 8: TESTING THE SPIRITS (EVEN THE TRENDY ONES)

Why Not Everything That Feels Spiritual Is From God

When "Spiritual" Stops Being Safe

Let's be honest: not everything that feels spiritual is good for your soul.

Not every voice that says "Jesus" is pointing you to Him. Not every worship lyric that gives you goosebumps is grounded in truth. Not every "word from the Spirit" is actually from the Spirit of God.

You've heard the phrases:

- "This really resonated with me."
- "I had such peace, so it must've been God."
- "The Spirit gave me a word for you."
- "God wouldn't divide us—He just wants love."

They sound inspiring. They feel validating. They seem unifying. But here's the problem: **feelings aren't filters for truth.**

Scripture is.

"Beloved, do not believe every spirit, but test the spirits to see whether they are from God…" — 1 John 4:1

You were never meant to passively accept every message that makes you feel good. You were called to discern.

Counterfeit Unity Wants You Passive

Counterfeit unity thrives when you stop testing. It whispers:

- *"Don't ask questions—you'll sound divisive."*
- *"Don't raise concerns—you're being fear-based."*
- *"Don't share convictions—you're being judgmental."*

Over time, the standard shifts: if it feels good, it must be good. If it sounds spiritual, it must be true.

But Scripture never teaches emotional safety as the test of truth. Instead:

"Test everything; hold fast what is good." — 1 Thessalonians 5:21

Discernment isn't optional—it's obedience.

Why This Culture Is So Easy to Fall Into

Let's admit it: some of us grew up in churches where theology was used as a weapon. Where leaders crushed people with rules but never lifted them with grace. Where "discernment" meant suspicion, not wisdom.

So we swung the pendulum. We said:

- "I just want something authentic."
- "I'm tired of religious rules."
- "Let's just keep it real."

That desire for authenticity is good. But counterfeit unity hijacks it. It turns emotional resonance into a substitute for revelation.

In today's trend-driven spirituality:

- Emotions outweigh Scripture.
- Platforms matter more than pastors.
- Emotional safety trumps biblical soundness.

But spiritual hype doesn't equal spiritual health.

As J.I. Packer warned: *"A half-truth masquerading as the whole truth becomes a complete untruth."*

Discernment Isn't Cynicism—It's Discipleship

Some people hear "test the spirits" and think it means becoming suspicious of everything. But discernment isn't cynicism—it's discipleship.

- The Bereans were called "noble" because they examined the Scriptures daily to see if Paul's teaching was true (Acts 17:11).
- Hebrews 5:14 says maturity comes from "constant practice to distinguish good from evil."
- Paul warned that even Satan disguises himself as an angel of light (2 Corinthians 11:14).

Discernment is not division. It's devotion. It's how you love wisely, protect the Gospel, and grow into maturity.

The Spirit of Truth vs. the Spirit of Trend

John gives us a clear test:

"By this you know the Spirit of God: every spirit that confesses that Jesus Christ has come in the flesh is from God." — 1 John 4:2

There are only two spirits at work in the world:

- One lifts up Jesus as Savior and Lord.
- The other reduces Him to a metaphor, a vibe, or a lifestyle brand.

So here's your filter:

- Does this message point to Christ as the only way—or just one way?
- Does it align with God's Word—or just your feelings?
- Does it call you to repentance—or just to resonate?

If not, it's not from God.

Why You'll Be Labeled "Divisive"

Here's the cost: if you test what's trendy, you'll be called judgmental, fear-based, too intense, or "not walking in love."

But testing the spirits isn't harsh—it's holy.

Francis Schaeffer put it this way: *"Truth carries confrontation. Truth demands confrontation. Loving confrontation, but confrontation nevertheless."*

The church doesn't need more sensations. It needs clarity.

Discernment Is the Church's Immune System

Imagine your body without an immune system. Everything that looks good, smells good, or feels good gets in—and starts killing you from the inside.

That's what happens when the church loses discernment.

Without testing the spirits:

- Charisma gets mistaken for calling.
- False teaching sneaks into playlists and pulpits.
- Spiritual trends replace spiritual truth.

Discernment is how the church stays healthy. And it starts with you—not just pastors or leaders.

Think About This

- Are you chasing what feels spiritual—or what is actually biblical?
- Are you building your life on God's voice—or your own inner aura?
- Are you brave enough to test the spirits—especially the ones that make you feel good?

Because if Satan disguises himself as an angel of light, you can't afford to turn your brain off just because someone says, "God gave me a word."

If it contradicts God's Word, it doesn't matter how spiritual it feels—it's not from God.

Conclusion: Testing Is Love

Testing the spirits isn't about being harsh. It's about being holy. It's not about suspicion—it's about salvation.

Counterfeit unity thrives in fog. Real unity thrives in clarity.

And clarity comes when you test everything by the Word of God.

If testing the spirits is essential, then we need to recognize the red flags of spirituality that poses as truth. In the next chapter, we'll look at how mysticism, emotion, and trendy "unity" cloak themselves in Christian language—and how to spot the difference.

CHAPTER 9: WHEN SPIRITUALITY POSES AS TRUTH

How Trendy Mysticism and Emotionalism Infiltrate the Church Under the Banner of Unity

---

The Rise of "Spiritual"

Walk into a coffee shop and you'll overhear it. Scroll TikTok and you'll see it. Sit in a small group and you might even feel it.

"I'm spiritual, but not religious." "I don't like doctrine—I just want Jesus." "I feel God in the energy of the room."

It sounds humble. It sounds authentic. It even sounds Christian. But here's the problem: **spirituality isn't always truth.**

In fact, some of the most dangerous lies don't come dressed as lies. They come dressed as light, wrapped in worship lyrics, or whispered in the language of love and unity.

Why This Hits So Close to Home

For Gen-Z and Millennials, spirituality is attractive because it feels flexible. It doesn't demand definitions. It doesn't draw boundaries. It doesn't divide.

- You can light a candle and call it prayer.
- You can meditate and call it worship.
- You can chase goosebumps in a worship set and call it the Spirit.

And because counterfeit unity has already trained us to avoid confrontation, we rarely stop to ask: *Is this actually from God—or just from me?*

The Fog of Mysticism

Mysticism isn't new. It's as old as Eden, where the serpent whispered, *"You will be like God."* (Genesis 3:5)

But today, it's been rebranded for a digital generation. It shows up in phrases like:

- "Find your center."
- "Tap into the divine spark within."
- "The universe is speaking to you."

And here's the subtle twist: these ideas often get baptized in Christian language. Instead of "the universe," we say "God." Instead of "energy," we say "Spirit." Instead of "alignment," we say "anointing."

But the substance hasn't changed. It's still self-focused, experience-driven, and detached from the authority of Scripture.

As Richard Kyle warns: *"New Age spirituality often infiltrates by spiritualizing Christian terms, while divorcing them from biblical theology."*

Emotionalism Masquerading as the Spirit

Mysticism isn't the only counterfeit. Emotionalism is its twin.

In many churches, the measure of God's presence has quietly shifted from **truth proclaimed** to **feelings produced.**

- If the lights are low and the music swells, it must be God.
- If the crowd is crying, it must be the Spirit.
- If I feel peace, it must be His will.

But here's the danger: **feelings are real, but they're not always reliable.**

- Jonah felt justified running from God.
- The disciples felt despair when Jesus was crucified.
- The Pharisees felt righteous when they condemned Him.

Feelings can confirm truth, but they can also deceive. When emotion becomes the foundation, discernment disappears.

Unity as the Cover Story

Why do mysticism and emotionalism spread so easily in the church? Because they hide under the banner of unity.

- "Don't question the experience—you'll divide us."
- "Don't critique the teaching—it's unifying people."
- "Don't test the spirits—you'll kill the vibe."

But unity built on untested spirituality isn't unity—it's surrender. It's the church lowering its immune system and inviting in every virus that feels inspiring.

As J.I. Packer warned: *"A half-truth masquerading as the whole truth becomes a complete untruth."*

The Spirit of Truth vs. the Spirit of Trend

John gives us a clear test:

"By this you know the Spirit of God: every spirit that confesses that Jesus Christ has come in the flesh is from God." — 1 John 4:2

There are only two spirits at work in the world:

- One lifts up Jesus as Savior and Lord.
- The other reduces Him to a metaphor, a vibe, or a lifestyle brand.

So here's the filter:

- Does this message exalt Christ—or just your feelings?
- Does it align with Scripture—or just your preferences?
- Does it call you to repentance—or just to resonate?

If not, it's not the Spirit of God.

Why You'll Be Called "Divisive"

Here's the cost: if you test what's trendy, you'll be labeled judgmental, fear-based, or "not walking in love."

But testing the spirits isn't harsh—it's holy.

The church doesn't need more sensations. It needs clarity. It doesn't need more chill. It needs conviction.

Discernment Is the Church's Immune System

Imagine your body without an immune system. Everything that looks good, smells good, or feels good gets in—and starts killing you from the inside.

That's what happens when the church loses discernment.

Without testing the spirits:

- Charisma gets mistaken for calling.
- Mysticism replaces theology.
- Emotional highs replace holiness.

And slowly, the church drifts—not into atheism, but into a spirituality that feels Christian while denying Christ.

Think About This

- Are you chasing what feels spiritual—or what is actually biblical?
- Are you building your life on God's Word—or your own inner aura?
- Are you brave enough to test the spirits—especially the ones that make you feel good?

Because if Satan disguises himself as an angel of light (2 Corinthians 11:14), then you can't afford to turn your brain off just because something feels inspiring.

Conclusion: Don't Confuse Fog for Fire

Mysticism and emotionalism promise unity, but they deliver confusion. They offer belonging, but without boundaries. They offer spirituality, but without the Spirit of Truth.

Counterfeit unity thrives in fog. Real unity thrives in fire—the fire of God's Word, the fire of His Spirit, the fire of truth that purifies and refines.

Don't confuse fog for fire. Don't settle for vibes when you've been offered victory.

If counterfeit spirituality poses as truth, then what does real unity look like? In the next chapter, we'll see how unity in Christ is not a vibe, not a trend, not a performance—but a covenant rooted in His cross.

CHAPTER 10: REAL UNITY IN CHRIST

Why Biblical Unity Isn't a Sentiment—It's a Covenant

The Longing That Won't Go Away

Every generation longs for unity. We want to belong. We want to be known. We want to be part of something bigger than ourselves. That longing is not a flaw—it's a fingerprint. It's evidence that we were made for community, not isolation.

But here's the problem: when we try to satisfy that longing apart from Christ, we end up with counterfeits. We settle for vibes, slogans, and emotional highs. We trade conviction for consensus. We confuse silence with peace.

And yet, the longing doesn't go away. Because it was never meant to be satisfied by "All is One" mysticism, or by the idol of inclusion, or by emotional atmospheres. It was meant to be satisfied in Christ.

Jesus' Prayer for Unity

On the night before being arrested, which led to His crucifixion, Jesus prayed for His disciples—and for us:

"I do not ask for these only, but also for those who will believe in me through their word, that they may all be one, just as you, Father, are in me, and I in you, that they also may be in us, so that the world may believe that you have sent me." — John 17:20–21

Notice what He prayed for:

- Not a shallow peace.

- Not agreement on every secondary issue.
- Not a unity built on vibes or slogans.

He prayed for a unity that mirrors the very relationship between Father and Son. A unity that is relational, covenantal, and supernatural.

As D.A. Carson explains: *"The unity Jesus prays for is not merely institutional or sentimental, but a unity grounded in shared truth about who He is."*

Real unity is not a marketing strategy. It's a miracle.

Unity Through the Cross

Here's the paradox: unity doesn't come by avoiding conflict. It comes through the greatest conflict in history—the cross.

Paul writes: "He Himself is our peace, who has made us both one and has broken down in His flesh the dividing wall of hostility." — Ephesians 2:14

Jesus didn't create unity by ignoring sin. He created unity by confronting it—absorbing it in His own body, reconciling us to God and to one another.

That means real unity is not sentimental. It's sacrificial. It's not built on affirmation. It's built on atonement.

What Real Unity Looks Like

Let's be clear about the difference between counterfeit unity and real unity:

Counterfeit Unity	Real Unity in Christ
Built on feelings	Built on truth
Afraid of disagreement	Willing to engage with conviction
Avoids truth for peace	Speaks truth in love
Prioritizes comfort	Prioritizes holiness
Treats Jesus as a mascot	Worships Jesus as Lord
Consensus-driven	Christ-centered

Dietrich Bonhoeffer put it this way: *"Christian community is not an ideal we must realize, but rather a reality created by God in Christ in which we may participate."*

Unity is not something we manufacture. It's something we receive.

Unity Requires Repentance

Here's the part our culture resists: real unity requires repentance.

Counterfeit unity says: "Come as you are, and stay as you are."
Jesus says: "Come as you are, but don't stay as you are."

- To the woman caught in adultery: *"Go, and sin no more."*
- To Zacchaeus: *"Salvation has come"*—*after radical repentance.*
- To the rich young ruler: *"Sell everything and follow me."*

Inclusion was the door. Repentance was the path. Transformation was the destination.

Unity without repentance is just performance. Real unity begins when we stop deflecting, confess, and walk humbly under grace.

Unity That Witnesses to the World

Jesus prayed that our unity would be a testimony: *"...so that the world may believe that you have sent me."*

That means unity is not just for us. It's for the watching world.

When the church is divided, the world shrugs. But when the church is united in truth and love, the world takes notice. Because it's not natural. It's supernatural.

As Francis Schaeffer said: *"The final apologetic is the observable love of true Christians for one another."*

Think About This

- Am I part of a Christian community—or just a Christian aesthetic?
- Do I want harmony more than holiness?
- Have I surrendered to Christ—or just blended in?

Because you don't find real unity by chasing agreement. You find it by bowing before the same Lord.

Conclusion: The Unity We Were Made For

Counterfeit unity is fragile. It collapses under pressure. It silences truth to preserve peace. It offers belonging without transformation.

But real unity in Christ is different. It's not a vibe. It's not a brand. It's not a performance. It's a covenant.

It's the unity Jesus prayed for. It's the unity the cross purchased.

It's the unity the Spirit sustains.

And it's the unity the world desperately needs to see.

If real unity is found in Christ, then we need to rediscover what real love looks like. Because love is the glue of unity—but only if it's the kind of love that doesn't lie. That's where we turn next.

CHAPTER 11: LOVE THAT DOESN'T LIE

When "Love and Acceptance" Stops Looking Like Jesus

The Word Everyone Applauds

If there's one word our culture still celebrates without hesitation, it's **love**.

Politicians campaign on it. Influencers hashtag it. Churches preach it. Songs repeat it. And for Gen-Z and Millennials, love has become the highest virtue—the one thing no one dares to question.

But here's the problem: **love has been redefined.**

In the world of counterfeit unity, love no longer means seeking someone's ultimate good. It means avoiding their discomfort. It no longer points people to Jesus. It points people back to themselves.

This new definition of love is the crown jewel of counterfeit unity. It's the emotional glue that holds the illusion together—the reason people go silent, the reason truth gets blurred, the reason correction feels like cruelty.

But if your love never speaks truth, it's not love. It's fear.

When "Love" Gets Rewritten

You've heard the slogans:

- "Love and accept everyone."
- "Love is love."
- "If you love me, you'll affirm me."

They sound noble. They sound compassionate. They even sound Christlike. But behind them is an entire worldview—one that feels good on the surface but collapses under biblical light.

In this new paradigm:

- **Sin** is reframed as "living your truth."
- **Conviction** is labeled as shame.
- **Repentance** is replaced by "alignment."
- **Jesus** becomes a symbol of radical acceptance, not a Savior who demands surrender.

This version of love claims to look like Jesus—but it won't flip tables. It won't warn Pharisees. It won't call sinners to "go and sin no more."

And that's the problem. Because the real Jesus did all of that.

The Jesus Who Loved With Truth

The Jesus of the Bible loved people deeply—but His love never lied.

- He welcomed sinners, but He also told them to repent.
- He healed the broken, but He also called them to holiness.
- He forgave freely, but He also demanded transformation.

The same Christ who wept over Jerusalem also called religious leaders "whitewashed tombs." The same God who welcomed sinners with open arms also spoke of hell more than anyone else in Scripture.

Jesus loved with clarity. He healed with holiness. He never separated grace from truth—and neither should we.

As Rosaria Butterfield puts it: *"Love that goes silent in the face of sin is not love. It is cowardice."*

Love That Never Offends Will Never Save

Imagine someone's house is on fire. They're asleep inside. You walk by, smell the smoke... but instead of waking them, you leave a scented candle on the porch with a Post-it that says, *"You are enough."*

Is that compassion?

That's the logic of counterfeit love. It's kind until it's needed. It's soft until it's dangerous. It's popular—but powerless.

Real love kicks the door down. Real love risks offense. Real love says what must be said, even when it costs you everything.

As Dr. Michael Kruger warns: *"The church is not loving when it offers a soft pillow to people heading toward destruction."*

And here's the kicker. Verses in the Bible that speak of love are wonderful, for they point to the character of God. But if you only pick verses that speak of love and avoid everything else, you have a limited view of God and of reality. Sin is real, and God demands repentance.

Don't Let Fear Masquerade as Kindness

Here's where it gets personal.

- Have you stayed silent about hard truths to keep people liking you?
- Have you watched someone drift from Christ while applauding their "journey"?
- Have you confused being agreeable with being faithful?

If so, you've felt the pull of counterfeit love.

But silence isn't always love. Sometimes it's fear in a flattering disguise.

Jesus didn't love people by protecting their feelings. He loved them by rescuing their souls—even when it cut deep.

Real Love Draws Lines

The Bible is clear:

- *"Those whom I love, I rebuke and discipline."* (Revelation 3:19)
- *"Love does not rejoice at wrongdoing, but rejoices with the truth."* (1 Corinthians 13:6)
- *"Faithful are the wounds of a friend."* (Proverbs 27:6)

God's love isn't allergic to confrontation. It's precisely His love that drives Him to correct, refine, and rescue.

That's not harsh. That's holy.

Love and Accept Everyone?

"Love and accept everyone."
It's the favorite mantra of Counterfeit Unity. It sounds kind, inclusive, and unifying. But is that actually what Jesus did?

Jesus loved everyone—**deeply, sacrificially, without exception.**

"For God so loved the world that He gave His only begotten Son, that whoever believes in Him shall not perish but have eternal life." (John 3:16)

That's the kind of love that bleeds for others. The kind that enters human pain, not to affirm it, but to redeem it.

But **love and acceptance are not the same thing.**
Jesus didn't come to hand out validation; He came to call people to repentance. He welcomed sinners, yes—but He never affirmed their sin. He invited the broken, but He didn't bless their rebellion.

He rebuked the Pharisees for hypocrisy.
He warned false teachers that judgment was coming.
He called His followers to deny themselves, not indulge themselves.

And He said clearly:

"Not everyone who says to Me, 'Lord, Lord,' will enter the kingdom of heaven, but only the one who does the will of My Father who is in heaven."
(Matthew 7:21)

That doesn't sound like unconditional acceptance. It sounds like a holy invitation—one that demands transformation.

In the book of Revelation, Jesus speaks to churches that had compromised truth in the name of tolerance. To the church in Thyatira, He says:

"I have this against you, that you tolerate that woman Jezebel, who calls herself a prophetess and is teaching and seducing my servants."
(Revelation 2:20)

In other words: **love does not mean tolerance of lies.**

The New Testament doesn't shy away from this tension.
• Paul wrote, "As for a person who stirs up division, after warning him once and then twice, have nothing more to do with him." *(Titus 3:10)*
• John warned, "If anyone comes to you and does not bring this teaching, do not receive him into your house." *(2 John 1:10)*
• Jesus Himself told His disciples to beware of false prophets. *(Matthew 7:15)*

That's not cruelty—it's clarity.
Love without truth isn't compassion; it's complicity.

As theologian John Stott once said:

"Our love grows soft if it is not strengthened by truth, and our truth grows hard if it is not softened by love."

Counterfeit Unity takes only half of that equation. It keeps love, discards truth, and calls the result compassion. But that's not what Jesus modeled.
Real love doesn't leave people where they are—it leads them home.

Reflection

This is why Counterfeit Unity feels so powerful—it borrows the language of love but empties it of holiness. It preaches acceptance without repentance, belonging without belief, grace without truth. But the gospel refuses to separate the two. Jesus' love saves because it transforms. His welcome is real—but it always comes with a call: *"Follow Me."*

The moment love stops calling us to change, it stops being love at all.
And that's where unity dies—when comfort replaces conversion, and truth becomes optional.

Let Love Get Its Spine Back

If we want real unity, we have to recover real love.

A love that can cry and confront. A love that embraces and exhorts. A love that dares to be uncomfortable—because it dares to be like Christ.

Don't settle for fake peace. Don't settle for shallow love.

If your love never says hard things, maybe it's not love—it's fear dressed in compassion's clothing.

As Os Guinness reminds us: *"A truth that's not spoken is not a truth that saves."*

Think About This

- Do I love people enough to tell them the truth?
- Have I confused affirmation with compassion?
- Am I willing to risk being misunderstood in order to be faithful?

Because love that never offends will never save.

Conclusion: The Love That Holds Unity Together

Counterfeit unity thrives on counterfeit love—love that lies to keep the peace. But real unity is held together by real love—love that tells the truth, even when it hurts.

This is the love Jesus modeled. The love that flips tables and washes feet. The love that comforts the broken and confronts the proud. The love that doesn't just accept you as you are, but transforms you into who you were meant to be.

That's the love that doesn't lie. That's the love that builds real unity.

If love is the glue of unity, then truth is the foundation. But what exactly do we unify on? What truths are non-negotiable for the people of God? In the next chapter, we'll look at five ancient anchors—the Five Solas—that have held the church together for centuries.

CHAPTER 12: WHAT DO WE UNIFY ON?

How the Five Solas Anchor Real Unity in Christ

The Question That Won't Go Away

We've spent this book exposing the counterfeits. We've seen how counterfeit unity thrives on vibes, slogans, emotional highs, and shallow inclusion. We've seen how it silences truth, kills discernment, and redefines love.

But now the question presses in: **If counterfeit unity is hollow, what do we actually unify on?**

Because unity for unity's sake isn't enough. We need something stronger than feelings, deeper than slogans, and more enduring than cultural trends. We need a foundation that doesn't shift when the world does.

For centuries, Christians have summarized that foundation in five short phrases. They're called the **Five Solas**—Latin for "onlys." They existed in the early church and were re-forged in the fires of the Reformation, but they're not dusty relics. They're living anchors. They're the bedrock of real unity.

And if we want to recover unity that lasts, we need to return to them.

1. Sola Scriptura — Scripture Alone

Counterfeit unity says: *"Truth is whatever resonates."* Real unity says: *"Truth is what God has spoken."*

"All Scripture is breathed out by God and profitable for teaching, for reproof, for correction, and for training in righteousness." — 2 Timothy 3:16

Unity begins with a shared authority. If Scripture is optional, then unity is impossible. Because without a common foundation, we're just drifting near each other, pretending we're together.

This doesn't mean we'll agree on every secondary issue. But it does mean we agree on this: **God's Word is the final word.** Not culture. Not feelings. Not influencers. Not algorithms.

When we filter Scripture through our experiences, we end up with a thousand different "truths." But when we filter our experiences through Scripture, we find one truth that unites us.

---

2. Solus Christus — Christ Alone

Counterfeit unity says: *"All paths lead to God."* Real unity says: *"There is one Mediator—Jesus Christ."*

"For there is one God, and there is one mediator between God and men, the man Christ Jesus." — 1 Timothy 2:5

In a world of spiritual remixing, Jesus often gets reduced to a mascot for whatever cause we care about. He's portrayed as a moral teacher, a revolutionary, or a vibe. But the Jesus of Scripture is not a lifestyle brand. He is Lord.

Unity is not built on vague spirituality. It's built on a Person—the crucified and risen Christ. If we're not united in Him, we're not united at all.

---

3. Sola Gratia — Grace Alone

Counterfeit unity says: *"You're enough. Just be authentic."* Real unity says: *"You're not enough—but God's grace is."*

"For by grace you have been saved through faith. And this is not your own doing; it is the gift of God." — Ephesians 2:8

Grace levels the playing field. It reminds us that none of us earned our way in. We're not united because we're impressive. We're united because we're forgiven.

Without grace, churches turn into performance clubs, where people compete for approval. But grace kills comparison. It creates humility. It reminds us that we're all beggars at the same table, fed by the same mercy.

---

4. Sola Fide — Faith Alone

Counterfeit unity says: *"Just try harder. Do better. Prove yourself."* Real unity says: *"We are justified by faith apart from works."*

"For we hold that one is justified by faith apart from works of the law." — Romans 3:28

Faith is the great equalizer. It humbles the achiever and lifts up the failure. It reminds us that salvation isn't about what we do for God—it's about what God has done for us in Christ.

And here's the beauty: shared faith creates family. You don't have to look the same, vote the same, or come from the same background. If you trust the same Savior, you're united.

---

5. Soli Deo Gloria — To the Glory of God Alone

Counterfeit unity says: *"This is about us—our brand, our platform, our vibe."* Real unity says: *"This is about God."*

"So, whether you eat or drink, or whatever you do, do all to the glory of God." — 1 Corinthians 10:31

This is the ultimate anchor. Unity isn't about making us look good. It's about making God look glorious.

When God's glory is the goal, we stop competing for attention. We stop performing for likes. We stop building unity around personalities, platforms, or aesthetics. We start living for something eternal.

Why the Five Solas Matter for Unity

The Five Solas aren't just theological slogans. They're the difference between counterfeit unity and real unity.

- **Without Scripture Alone**, unity drifts into relativism.
- **Without Christ Alone**, unity dissolves into pluralism.
- **Without Grace Alone**, unity collapses into performance.
- **Without Faith Alone**, unity fractures into pride.
- **Without God's Glory Alone**, unity shrinks into self-promotion.

But with them, unity becomes unshakable. Because it's not built on us. It's built on Him.

Think About This

- What's holding your friendships together—shared truth, or just shared vibes?
- What's holding your church together—Christ, or just culture?
- What's holding your faith together—God's Word, or your feelings?

Because unity built on anything less than the Five Solas will eventually collapse.

Conclusion: Anchored in the Only Foundation That Lasts

Counterfeit unity is easy. It's cheap. It's fragile.

Real unity is costly. It's rooted in truth. It's anchored in Christ. It's sustained by grace. It's received by faith. And it's lived for the glory of God.

This is the unity Jesus prayed for. This is the unity the cross purchased. This is the unity the Spirit sustains.

And this is the unity the world desperately needs to see.

We've seen the counterfeits. We've traced their roots. We've exposed their costs. And we've rediscovered the foundation of real unity. Now the question is: what will you do with it?

EPILOGUE: WHAT WE'VE SEEN— AND WHAT COMES NEXT

The Call to Reject Counterfeit Unity and Embrace the Costly Clarity of Christ

---

The Journey We've Taken

We've walked through the slogans, the vibes, the philosophies, and the illusions. We've seen how counterfeit unity whispers through culture:

- *"We're all one."*
- *"Love and accept everyone."*
- *"Don't divide over doctrine."*

We've unmasked how these mantras promise peace but deliver pressure, how they silence truth in the name of tolerance, and how they leave us with belonging that only lasts as long as no one speaks up.

We've traced the roots: Postmodernism, Deconstructionism, the "All is One" worldview. We've seen how counterfeit unity props itself up with emotional highs, how it infiltrates the church through mysticism and emotionalism, and how it kills discernment by making thinking feel dangerous.

And we've seen the idols: inclusion without repentance, love without truth, unity without Christ.

But we've also seen the way back.

We've seen that real unity is not a vibe, not a brand, not a performance. It's a covenant. It's anchored in truth, purchased at the cross, sustained by grace, received by faith, and lived for the glory of God.

The Cost of Clarity

Here's the truth: rejecting counterfeit unity will cost you.

- You may lose followers.
- You may lose the approval of your friend group.
- You may be labeled divisive, judgmental, or "too intense."

But clarity will give you something counterfeit unity never can: conviction, freedom, and Christ Himself.

Jesus never promised that following Him would make you popular. He promised it would make you free.

"You shall know the truth, and the truth shall set you free." — John 8:32

The Narrow Gate

Jesus warned us:

"Enter by the narrow gate. For the gate is wide and the way is easy that leads to destruction, and those who enter by it are many. For the gate is narrow and the way is hard that leads to life, and those who find it are few." — Matthew 7:13–14

Counterfeit unity is the wide gate. It's easy. It's popular. It feels safe. But it leads to destruction.

Real unity in Christ is the narrow gate. It's costly. It's countercultural. It demands repentance, conviction, and courage. But it leads to life.

A Call to This Generation

Gen-Z and Millennials—you are being discipled every day. By algorithms. By influencers. By slogans. By vibes.

But you don't have to drift. You don't have to settle for counterfeit unity. You don't have to silence your convictions to belong.

You can stand. You can speak. You can love with clarity. You can live with courage.

And when you do, you'll discover something deeper than vibes, stronger than slogans, and more lasting than trends. You'll discover the unity Jesus prayed for—the unity that testifies to the world that He is Lord.

What Comes Next

So here's the invitation:

- **Reject counterfeit unity.** Don't bow to the idol of inclusion without repentance. Don't confuse vibes with vision. Don't let silence masquerade as love.
- **Embrace costly clarity.** Speak the truth in love. Test the spirits. Love with a backbone. Stand on the Five Solas.
- **Live for Christ's glory.** Because unity isn't about us. It's about Him.

The world doesn't need another echo chamber. It doesn't need another curated community built on affirmation. It doesn't need another church that trades the cross for a couch.

The world needs to see the real thing.

Final Word

Counterfeit unity is easy. But it's empty. Real unity is costly. But it's eternal.

So choose clarity. Choose courage. Choose Christ.

Because in the end, the only unity that lasts is the unity that begins and ends with Him.

Closing Prayer

Lord Jesus Christ, You are the Truth that sets us free, the Love that never lies, and the Unity that holds Your people together.

Guard us from the counterfeits that promise peace but deliver emptiness. Give us courage to speak truth with grace, to love with conviction, and to walk in unity that is anchored in You alone.

May our lives bear witness to Your cross, our words reflect Your Word, and our communities shine with the glory of God alone.

Keep us faithful until the day we see You face to face, when every counterfeit will vanish and only Your kingdom will remain.

Amen.

ANNOTATED BIBLIOGRAPHY

1. Miller, Elliot. *A Crash Course on the New Age Movement.* Grand Rapids: Baker Book House, 1989. A concise yet thorough overview of New Age beliefs, tracing their roots in Eastern mysticism and occult philosophy. Miller exposes the incompatibility of New Age spirituality with biblical Christianity, offering clear apologetic responses. Supports your critique of "all is one" thinking and the need for discernment.

2. Groothuis, Douglas. *Unmasking the New Age.* Downers Grove, IL: InterVarsity Press, 1986. One of the earliest evangelical analyses of the New Age movement. Groothuis explains its worldview, practices, and infiltration into Western culture, then contrasts it with the gospel. Reinforces your argument that New Age spirituality replaces the personal God with an impersonal force.

3. Baer, Randall. *Inside the New Age Nightmare.* Lafayette, LA: Huntington House, 1989. A former New Age leader shares his testimony of coming to Christ. Baer's insider perspective reveals the spiritual deception and psychological manipulation common in New Age circles. His story illustrates the dangers of counterfeit unity built on mystical experience rather than truth.

4. Carson, D.A. *The Gagging of God: Christianity Confronts Pluralism.* Grand Rapids: Zondervan, 1996. A scholarly yet pastoral defense of the exclusivity of Christ in a pluralistic world. Carson addresses how Postmodernism undermines truth claims and how the church can respond with clarity and conviction. Directly supports your sections on the exclusivity of Christ and the dangers of affirming all beliefs equally.

5. McDowell, Josh, and Bob Hostetler. *The New Tolerance.* Wheaton, IL: Tyndale House, 1998. Explains how the modern redefinition of tolerance demands unconditional affirmation of all lifestyles and beliefs, silencing truth in the process. This aligns with your critique of unity that sacrifices truth for acceptance.

6. Guinness, Os. *Time for Truth: Living Free in a World of Lies, Hype, and Spin.* Grand Rapids: Baker Books, 2000. A short, powerful call to recover absolute truth in a culture of relativism. Guinness connects the loss of truth to the erosion of moral and spiritual integrity, echoing your warnings about counterfeit unity.

7. Keller, Timothy. *The Reason for God: Belief in an Age of Skepticism.* New York: Dutton, 2008. Engages respectfully with postmodern skepticism, defending the rationality and necessity of Christian faith. Keller's chapters on the exclusivity of Christ and the problem of relativism reinforce your apologetic approach.

8. Schaeffer, Francis A. *The God Who Is There.* Downers Grove, IL: InterVarsity Press, 1968. A foundational evangelical critique of modern and postmodern thought. Schaeffer shows how abandoning the God of the Bible leads to despair and meaninglessness. His framework undergirds your analysis of worldview foundations.

9. Wells, David F. *No Place for Truth: Or Whatever Happened to Evangelical Theology?* Grand Rapids: Eerdmans, 1993. Examines how cultural accommodation has weakened the church's theological convictions. Wells' call to recover doctrinal clarity parallels your emphasis on unity rooted in truth.

10. Stott, John. *The Contemporary Christian.* Downers Grove, IL: InterVarsity Press, 1992. Addresses how believers can engage culture without compromising biblical truth. Stott's balance of cultural awareness and theological fidelity mirrors your call for discernment in pursuing unity.

11. Packer, J.I. *Knowing God.* Downers Grove, IL: InterVarsity Press, 1973. A classic work on the character of God and the necessity of knowing Him personally through Christ. Packer's emphasis on God's holiness and love strengthens your argument for unity grounded in the gospel.

12. Zacharias, Ravi. *Jesus Among Other Gods.* Nashville: Word Publishing, 2000. Defends the uniqueness of Jesus against the claims of other religions. Zacharias' clear contrast between Christ and other spiritual leaders supports your insistence that unity must be built on the exclusive truth of the gospel.

FOR FURTHER READING

Understanding and Responding to Postmodernism & Relativism

- **D.A. Carson** – *The Gagging of God: Christianity Confronts Pluralism* A thorough defense of the exclusivity of Christ in a culture that treats all beliefs as equally valid.
- **Josh McDowell & Bob Hostetler** – *The New Tolerance* Explains how the modern redefinition of tolerance silences truth and undermines biblical conviction.
- **Os Guinness** – *Time for Truth: Living Free in a World of Lies, Hype, and Spin* A concise call to recover absolute truth in an age of relativism.
- **Francis A. Schaeffer** – *The God Who Is There* A classic evangelical critique of modern and postmodern thought, showing the necessity of God's truth.

Exposing and Answering the New Age Movement

- **Elliot Miller** – *A Crash Course on the New Age Movement* A clear overview of New Age beliefs and a biblical response.
- **Douglas Groothuis** – *Unmasking the New Age* Explains New Age philosophy and practices, contrasting them with the gospel.
- **Randall Baer** – *Inside the New Age Nightmare* A former New Age leader's testimony and theological critique of its deceptions.

Cultural Discernment & Guarding Against Syncretism

- **David F. Wells** – *No Place for Truth: Or Whatever Happened to Evangelical Theology?* Examines how cultural accommodation weakens the church's theological convictions.
- **John Stott** – *The Contemporary Christian* Offers guidance on engaging culture without compromising biblical truth.

The Exclusivity and Sufficiency of Christ

- **J.I. Packer** – *Knowing God* A classic on the character of God and the necessity of knowing Him through Christ alone.
- **Ravi Zacharias** – *Jesus Among Other Gods* Defends the uniqueness of Jesus against the claims of other religions.
- **Timothy Keller** – *The Reason for God: Belief in an Age of Skepticism* Engages respectfully with skeptics, defending the rationality and necessity of Christian faith.

Made in the USA
Coppell, TX
18 February 2026

72033366R00046